JACK and Jill

Flip-Side Rhymes

from the
perspective of JACK

by Christopher Harbo
illustrated by Colin Jack

PICTURE WINDOW BOOKS
a capstone imprint

Jack and

Jill

went up the hill

to fetch
a pail
of water.

Jack fell down
and broke his crown,

and Jill came tumbling after.

NOW FLIP THE BOOK
TO GET ANOTHER SIDE OF THE RHYME.

Picture Window Books are published by Capstone.
1710 Roe Crest Drive, North Mankato, Minnesota 56003
www.capstoneyoungreaders.com

Library of Congress Cataloging-in-Publication Data
Harbo, Christopher L.
  Jack and Jill flip-side rhymes / by Christopher Harbo ; illustrated by Colin Jack.
    pages cm. — (Nonfiction picture books. Flip-side nursery rhymes)
  Summary: "Color illustrations and simple text give the original Jack and Jill
nursery rhyme, along with a fractured version from the perspective of Jill"—
Provided by publisher.
ISBN 978-1-4795-6008-0 (paper over board)
ISBN 978-1-4795-6986-1 (ebook PDF)
1. Nursery rhymes. 2. Children's poetry. 3. Upside-down books—Specimens.
[1. Nursery rhymes. 2. Upside-down books.] I. Jack, Colin, illustrator.
II. Mother Goose. III. Title.
  PZ8.3.H19669Jac 2015
  398.2—dc23 [E]   2014032213

Editor: Gillia Olson
Designer: Ashlee Suker
Art Director: Nathan Gassman
Production Specialist: Laura Manthe
The illustrations in this book were created digitally.

Printed in the United States of America in North Mankato, Minnesota.
092014   008482CGS15

JACK and Jill

FLIP-SIDE Rhymes

from the perspective of Jill

by Christopher Harbo

illustrated by Colin Jack

PICTURE WINDOW BOOKS
a capstone imprint

Jack shoved Jill

as they climbed the hill,

4

so she kicked him
in the britches.

7

Her laces caught on the pail he brought.

10

crowns sport stitches!

NOW FLIP THE BOOK
TO GET ANOTHER SIDE OF THE RHYME.

other titles in this series:

JACK and Jill
Flip-Side Rhymes

Little BO PEEP
Flip-Side Rhymes

Little Miss MUFFET
Flip-Side Rhymes